Hymns and Letters

Ann Griffiths

The hymns translated by Alan Gaunt
Music selected and edited by Alan Luff
The letters translated and edited by Alan Luff
Introduction to the life and work of Ann Griffiths by Kathryn Jenkins

Stainer & Bell

First published in 1999 by
Stainer & Bell Limited, PO Box 110, Victoria House,
23 Gruneisen Road, London N3 1DZ, England.

British Library Cataloging-in-Publication Data
A catalogue record for this book is available from the British Library

ISBN 0 85249 854 3

Printed in Great Britain by Galliards, Great Yarmouth

Contents

Publisher's Foreword

Though little known in her lifetime, Ann Griffiths is now widely regarded as being among the leading hymnwriters of Wales. She is a major figure whose work speaks strongly to a contemporary audience at a time of growing sensitivity to Christian spirituality in its many and varied forms, and to the often unacknowledged role of women in the life and history of the church.

Alan Gaunt's English translations of her hymns from the original Welsh are a significant addition to the growing literature that now fosters an awareness of her achievement. They were first published alongside his collected hymn texts, 1991-96, *Always from Joy* (Stainer & Bell, 1997), where they were praised by A. M. Allchin for their unique combination of singability with fidelity to their source. It therefore seems fitting that they should also be made available separately, with musical settings both traditional and contemporary that might encourage their wider use in congregational singing and worship.

In addition to selecting and editing a wealth of tunes for this purpose, the Revd Canon Alan Luff, formerly Precentor of Westminster Abbey and a noted authority on Welsh hymnody, has also translated and edited Ann Griffiths' eight surviving letters, to make a rounded collection that will introduce her corpus of writing to non-specialist readers wishing to learn more about the subject. An essay by Dr Kathryn Jenkins of the University of Wales, placing Ann in the context of her life and times, completes the picture.

Long held in high esteem in her homeland, Ann Griffiths is a figure whose reputation, like ripples on the sea, spreads ever outwards as new generations discover and appreciate the uniqueness of her writing. With this publication, it is hoped to carry the message of her lively word to English-speaking readers and worshippers not only in her native Wales, but wherever else there also flourishes an appetite for vigorous, thought-provoking and uplifting hymnody.

The Life and Work of Ann Griffiths

Nearly two hundred years after her premature death aged twenty-nine in August 1805 at a remote farmhouse in mid-Wales, much of the life and work of Ann Griffiths remains an enigma. As R. S. Thomas reminds us, she was 'the poor girl from the village/Without learning', of whom we neither know the exact date of her birth or death, and whose small body of work remained unpublished during her lifetime. In Wales she is profoundly cherished for the romance of her brief life, and the virtually inexplicable quality of her literature. Yet at the end of the twentieth century her strongly anti-materialistic themes, her intense focus on Christ, her superior application of scriptural allusion, her femininity and Celticity, her refreshing integrity and candour are attracting the interests of students of various traditions worldwide.

To be enthralled by Ann Griffiths (she was Ann Thomas until her marriage in 1804) is a spiritually energising experience, but it can also be intellectually tantalising. We have only one letter and one verse of a hymn in her handwriting; the rest has been variously redacted from oral tradition. We can only regret that there is no greater amount extant for study. It is also unfortunate that it is impossible to offer any reliable chronology for most of Ann's work. She dated two of her letters; we can surmise that another letter was written shortly after Easter 1802. In the case of her hymns we must rely on dated copies or contemporary accounts of sermons or events that influenced her.

The circumstances of Ann's life are rather unremarkable when compared to the remarkable spiritual life recounted in her work. As a woman at this time she was not expected to be either intelligent or noteworthy. She was nurtured within a devout, respectable, farming family. Devotion was a cornerstone of conduct, and parents and children were regular churchgoers. Her father, who was something of a folk poet, encouraged her literary interests. The family was prominent in its community. Ann in particular, it is said, enjoyed the energetic pursuits of dancing and partying in her youth. Her vivacious spirit and impressive appearance marked her out in company:

> ...she was of a gentle constitution, of fair and ruddy complexion, a rather high forehead, dark hair, taller of build than is usual for most women, cheerful eyes, and of quite a proud appearance, but despite this easily approached in enjoyable company.

Thus wrote her confidant and theological pedagogue, John Hughes in a belated memoir in 1846. Much has been made of Ann's supposed escapades in her youth in order to facilitate over-emphasis on her post-conversion evangelical holiness.

We are unable to pinpoint the exact time of her conversion. There is every likelihood that on Easter Monday 1796 she went to Llanfyllin, her nearest town, (she probably never travelled further than 15 miles from home throughout her lifetime) and joined a gathered congregation and heard Benjamin Jones of Pwllheli preaching. Months of seeking more profound assurances ensued. She was reluctant to leave the Established Church and join the Methodist Cause principally led by Thomas Charles of Bala that was increasingly capturing souls throughout

North Wales at this time, including members of her own family. Finally and probably having listened to Ishmael Jones of Llandinam, Ann joined the Methodist *Seiat*, that is 'Society', at Pontrobert. The seiat was a kind of group therapy where like-minded Methodists discussed and studied the scriptures, analysed their own experiences, and prayed together for their own and others' salvation. Ann's spirituality, however individualistic, thus found its touchstone in an experience shared by family and community.

Seven of the eight of Ann's extant letters were written to John Hughes of Pontrobert. The eighth was written to Elizabeth Evans, and is an acute account of the work of the Holy Spirit, and a dissection of Ann's deepest thoughts. It is only in recent years that critics have begun to estimate truly the quality of all her letters as religious prose. Through them we are able to eavesdrop on an incomplete dialogue, a correspondence that was mutually appreciated. They are subjective works that reveal Ann's total absorption in a life of prayer, praise and meditation. The expression of a young woman's spiritual experience in a letter was not new to Welsh literature. William Williams of Pantycelyn used the character of Martha Philopur in 1762 to sanction the conversion experience, to offer an apologia for the Enthusiasm of the Methodist Revival, and to validate both through scriptural reference. His work, however, was meant for the public domain. Ann's letters were only ever part of a one-to-one correspondence, 'since you know more about my story in all kinds of misery than does anyone else' (Letter 1). Some have suggested, probably incorrectly, that they may have been read at various Society meetings. In them we are given the occasional reference to contemporary events or the state of the Chapel at Pontrobert, although how reliable are Ann's estimates of the religious currents of her time is a matter for conjecture.

All the letters contain an outpouring of her joys and tribulations, and the exposition of various passages of scripture. They are an index to Ann's spiritual condition. She talks of 'our great wretchedness', (Letter 2) of 'my distress of mind, suffering as I do gnawing doubts' (Letter 3), 'a more pitiful state than is mine at the moment' (Letter 7). Her fourth letter is permeated with references to struggle as she grapples with the challenges of discipleship. Her fifth and sixth letters meditate on God's goodness and her utter helplessness without her Mediator:

> I am reverently ashamed, and rejoice in astonishment, at the thought that the one for whom it is a condescension to behold the things that are in heaven, has given himself to be an object of love to a creature as base as I. (Letter 5)

Her Calvinism is much to the fore, and her introspection may be disconcerting. Certainly many of Ann's apologists in successive generations have been ill at ease with her almost pathological emphasis on her perceived sins and shortcomings. It is possible that the ravages of tuberculosis, which more than likely accounted for her premature death following childbirth, and which was responsible for approximately a quarter of all deaths among the population at this time, heightened the effect of Calvinist theology on her psychological stability.

Ann's hymns have a unique place in Welsh literature. It was her maid, Ruth Evans, who went to Dolwar Fach in May 1801 and stayed until her marriage to John Hughes in May 1805, who recounted to her husband the verses sung with such abandon by her mistress around the farm. Both Ruth and Ann's memories were outstanding: oral tradition had enhanced them over the years. We can only hope that what we now know as the hymns of Ann Griffiths are as close as possible to their original extempore composition and performance.

The verses of Ann's hymns encompass a unique vitality and ardour. Through scriptural allusion, some three hundred references in all, poetics and providence join forces and eternity impinges on time. Ann moves easily along the timeline of *heilsgeschichte*. God saved the Chosen

Race; Paul encountered the resurrected Lord: all are one in her imaginary intertextual ahistoric world. The reader is sucked into a raging vortex where her clamour for salvation is heightened by her dramatic, superlative diction and her use of accumulative repetition:

> Boldly, I will come before him;
> his gold sceptre in his hand,
> points toward this favoured sinner:
> here, accepted, all can stand.
> I'll press onward, shouting, 'pardon',
> fall before my gracious Lord:
> mine the pardon, mine the cleansing,
> mine the bleaching in his blood. (Hymn 1)

Ann likens herself to Esther seeking deliverance for the Jews. Salvation is both ultimate and intimate, and her obviously metaphorical expression adds a sensuous physicality to the spiritual reality.

The most remarkable feature of Ann's hymns is their utter concentration on Christ's person. It is He Himself who has suffered, and intuitively, she realises this. His victory is her source of consolation and assurance. Beholding Him, in a Pauline sense, all else becomes mere distraction:

> he excels by far ten thousand
> splendid sights in time and space. (Hymn 12)

Her doctrinal grasp of the basic tenets of the Christian faith is stupefying as she expounds the Chalcedonian Definition:

> two natures in one Person,
> conjoined inseparably,
> distinct and not confounded,
> in perfect unity. (Hymn 6)

Semantically, Ann's paradoxes take us beyond the realm of human understanding.

There remain many unanswered questions regarding the life and work of Ann Griffiths, and in some respects it is this enigma that draws critics to her literature. She herself, however, discovered many answers to eternal questions. These solutions she described with outstanding incisiveness in her hymns, and she sought further explanation of them in her letters. Her life was so enhanced by her faith that she desired to tarry 'in his love through all my days'. Our lives are now enhanced by her release.

Lampeter
Eastertide 1999

Kathryn Jenkins

Brief Chronology

? April 1776	Ann is born, fourth of five children to John Evan and Jane Thomas of Dolwar Fach farm in the parish of Llanfihangel-yng-Ngwynfa, Montgomeryshire, mid-Wales.
21 April 1776	Ann baptised at Llanfihangel Church.
c.Early 1780s	Receives some elementary education from Ann Owen y Sais ('the Englishwoman') at nearby village of Dolanog.
c.1792	John, Ann's eldest brother, is the first family member to be converted to Methodism.
31 January 1794	Jane, Ann's 50-year-old mother, is buried in Llanfihangel churchyard. The 17-year-old Ann becomes the mistress of Dolwar Fach with care of her widowed father.
1795–1796	The Methodist Cause gains new momentum at Pontrobert. John Hughes is converted.
Easter Monday 1796	Ann, now c. 20, listens to Rev. Benjamin Jones of Pwllheli preaching at Llanfyllin – and thus begins her conversion and awakening.
Christmas 1796	Alone, Ann attends the parish church, whilst her brothers worship with the Methodists. Seeks counsel from the curate, whose demeanour repels her from the Church.
1797	Ann finally joins the Methodist gathering or *Seiat* (i.e. 'society') at Pontrobert, 4 miles away.
1799	John Hughes lodges at Dolwar Fach for some months whilst in charge of a local circulating school.
1800	Pontrobert Chapel is built.
28 November 1800	Ann's first extant letter is sent to John Hughes.
c.December 1800	John Hughes begins to copy Ann's letters into a notebook (National Library of Wales MS 5864).
17 February 1801	Ann's second extant letter to John Hughes.
May 1801	Ruth Evans, maid, arrives at Dolwar Fach.
1801–2?	Ann begins to compose hymns.
1802	John Hughes begins preaching on Easter Sunday. Ann makes reference in her sixth letter.
c.1802–3	Probable date for only letter in Ann's handwriting. Written to Ruth's sister, Elizabeth Evans at Guilsfield, near Welshpool (National Library of Wales MS 694D).
23 February 1804	John Evan Thomas, 67 years of age, buried in Llanfihangel churchyard.
October 1804	John Hughes begins a written copy of some of Ann's hymns (National Library of Wales MS 5863).
10 October 1804	Ann marries Thomas Griffiths of Meifod, of a well-to-do Methodist farming family, at Llanfihangel Church.
7 May 1805	John Hughes marries Ruth Evans at Llanfihangel Church. Ann and Thomas are present as witnesses.
13 July 1805	Ann gives birth to a baby girl, Elizabeth.
31 July 1805	Elizabeth is buried in Llanfihangel churchyard.
12 August 1805	Ann is buried in Llanfihangel churchyard, aged 29.

1806	Thomas Charles of Bala publishes Ann's hymns in *Casgliad o Hymnau* ('A Collection of Hymns').
1846	John Hughes publishes a short [slightly unreliable] biography of Ann in the second volume of *Y Traethodydd* ('The Essayist') together with copies made by him of some of their correspondences.

(Note: Much of the above information is based on the researches and extensive publications of E. Wyn James.)

Select Bibliography

Allchin, A. M. *Ann Griffiths: the Furnace and the Fountain.* University of Wales Press, Cardiff, 1987.

Allchin, A. M. *Praise Above All: Discovering the Welsh Tradition.* University of Wales Press, Cardiff, 1991.

Allchin, A. M. *God's Presence Makes the World.* Darton, Longman and Todd, London, 1997.

Coutts, James (ed.) *Homage to Ann Griffiths.* Church in Wales Publications, Penarth, 1986. Includes an introduction to and translation of the hymns by H. A. Hodges and a translation of the lecture 'Ann Griffiths: a literary survey' by Saunders Lewis (1965).

Gaunt, Alan. *Always from Joy: Hymn Texts 1991–1996.* Stainer & Bell, London, 1997.

James, E. Wyn. *Rhyfeddaf Fyth... Emynau a llythyrau Ann Griffiths.* Gregynog Press, Gregynog, 1998.

Jenkins, Kathryn. '"Songs of Praises": the Literary and Spiritual Qualities of the Hymns of William Williams and Ann Griffiths', *Hymn Society of Great Britain and Ireland Bulletin* 214, 1998.

Lewis, H. Elvet. *Sweet Singers of Wales: A Story of Welsh Hymns and their Authors.* Tentmaker Publications, Clonmel, 1994. [Originally published by Religious Tract Society, 1889.]

Luff, Alan. *Welsh Hymns and their Tunes.* Hope Publishing Company and Stainer & Bell, Carol Stream, Illinois, and London, 1990.

Morton, Mark. 'Questions of Eternal Significance: the Theology of Ann Griffiths (1776–1805)'. Unpublished M.A. Dissertation, University of Wales, Lampeter, 1998.

Ryan, John. *The Hymns of Ann Griffiths.* Tŷ ar y Graig, printed at Caernarfon, 1980.

The Hymns of Ann Griffiths

translated by Alan Gaunt
with tunes selected by Alan Luff

I dedicate these translations
to John Hoskins
who so generously gave me the books,

to Ed and Kate Hill who make it possible for us
to spend so many delightful times in Wales,

and to John Richards
through whose support and friendship
I have increasingly admired and loved
all things Welsh

Alan Gaunt

Introduction to the Tunes

It is far easier to select tunes for these translations of Ann Griffiths' hymns than it is for the original Welsh, particularly when, as so often, she is composing in the 8787D metre.

In Ann's day, singing in the congregation was unaccompanied and usually in unison. This gives the singers freedom to introduce additional syllables, especially a weak syllable as an upbeat to the line that begins with a strong syllable, as do all the lines in 8787D. When trying to include her hymns in modern hymn books, Welsh editors are caught between two possibilities: of altering the words to fit the modern conventions, or of commissioning tunes specially crafted to include the possibility of additional syllables. Such tunes have been written but have not won popularity.

In any case, there is no evidence that Ann Griffiths had a congregation in mind. Few shared her hymns. Her own singing, and her singing with Ruth Evans, would thus be in the style of the flourishing traditions of the folksong, and of the ballad and carol, and could be quite free. (The second chapter of my *Welsh Hymns and their Tunes* (1990) contains an introduction to all these issues, for those who would like to explore the subject in more detail.)

Alan Gaunt, on the other hand, in making his translations, has accepted the disciplines of the modern hymn writer, and used the strict form of the metres in line with modern conventions. So for this edition of the hymns the whole wealth of tunes in the few metres that Ann Griffiths used is open.

No one can be confident about the tunes that she would herself have sung. I have not attempted to search any out, beyond using one tune from the carol and ballad tradition that is in the right metre, and looking carefully at the older Welsh melodies that are now in the modern repertoire. These can in any case be deceptive, in that they are now in use in arrangements that bring them into line with the tunes of the great period of Welsh hymn-tune writing from the middle of the 19th century into the beginning of the 20th. I have not tried to turn the clock back by trying to produce 'authentic' versions, since the purpose of setting tunes to these translations is to have them sung. I have thus used the familiar versions of the older tunes together with some fine tunes from the great period of Welsh tune writing.

There are in other traditions great tunes in the metres that Ann Griffiths uses (in 8787D AUSTRIA and ABBOT'S LEIGH come to mind), and while some musicians may wish to use these simply in order to get these great words sung, I have judged that they import a strong accent counter to the words, and that where possible Welsh tunes serve her words best.

With so many tunes to be found in this 8787D metre it has been hard to feel that a definitive choice can be offered. There is in any case such a wide range of emotion in the words of some of the hymns that no one tune could cover them with complete satisfaction. There lies behind this the problem that we can never be sure which stanzas Ann Griffiths thought of as belonging to one another in a complete hymn. This ignorance of what her intentions might have been has encouraged me to put stanzas together to make a hymn (25–27 and 28–30), since it is not in our tradition to sing single verses except for very special reasons.

Many will feel that they would wish to try other choices of tunes, so as to bring out other aspects of the words. It is in the tradition of both Welsh and English hymn-singing that such changes should be made. I would plead, however, that such changes should not mean that only the very familiar tunes are sung; there are great riches in the lesser used Welsh repertoire. Further, I would urge that such freedom of choice does not lead to the ignoring of the new tunes that have been in three cases written with these words in mind. There is one of these that needs special mention. The Welsh sing 'See him stand among the myrtles' to the very well known CWM RHONDDA. My own conviction is that this has been an attempt to drown with marching sounds the sensual power of these words. I hope that the new tune EDERN, and the more traditional LLWYNBEDW that is also suggested, will allow those who sing the English version to penetrate deeper into the true power of the words.

This should be the final emphasis. Welsh singing in its native habitat, the chapel and the church rather than in the large gathering under a conductor, lives by the words, powerful though the tunes may be. In singing these hymns, do not drag, or be slovenly, but on the other hand, always give the words plenty of time to sing themselves.

Cardiff
April 1999

Alan Luff

TANYMARIAN *E. Stephen (1822-85)*

1 Here we find the tent of meeting

Translated from 'Dyma babell y cyfarfod' 8.7.8.7.D. Trochaic

Here we find the tent of meeting,
here the blood that reconciles;
here is refuge for the slayer,
here the remedy that heals;
here a place beside the Godhead
here the sinner's nesting place,
where, for ever, God's pure justice
greets us with a smiling face.

Sinner is my name, most shameful,
chief of all in sinfulness;
yet such wonder! in this temple,
finding God in quietness;
he fulfils his law completely,
the transgressor shares his feast,
God and humans cry 'sufficient!'
Jesus, Sacrificed, makes peace.

Boldly, I will come before him;
his gold sceptre in his hand,
points toward this favoured sinner:
here, accepted, all can stand.
I'll press onward, shouting, 'pardon',
fall before my gracious Lord:
mine the pardon, mine the cleansing,
mine the bleaching in his blood.

O, to come like smoke in columns
rising from this wilderness,
straight toward his throne to see him
seated with unfrowning face;
without end, without beginning,
witness to the one in three,
making known the threefold glory,
True Amen, who sets us free.

For verse 3, lines 1–4, see Esther 4:9–5:3. *Even the Queen can only enter the presence of the King if he extends his sceptre towards her; otherwise the punishment is death.*

NEW BEGINNINGS

Roy Hopp (1951-)

Reprinted by permission of the composer

2 See, an open door before me

Translated from 'O'm blaen mi wela ddrws agored' 8.7.8.7.D. Trochaic

See, an open door before me,
means of total victory,
through the gifts the willing Servant
gained by his humility;
principalities are vanquished,
dominations disarrayed;
now captivity is captive,
through the sacrifice he made.*

My sad soul recalls the battle,
leaping up in ecstasy,
as I see the law exalted,
great transgressors going free;
life's great author has been buried,
Mighty Resurrection dies;
peace eternal is established,
earth united to the skies!

He ascends who once descended,
all his work is finished here;
heaven's gates, heads high with wonder,
welcome him as he draws near;
doors are opened, choirs revere him,
God in flesh, at journey's end,
hears his Father's invitation,
takes the seat at his right hand.

All I need through surging waters,
all I need through raging fire;
O, my soul, to cling for ever,
cling to him, my life's desire.
On Arabia's tangled pathways
plagued by foes increasingly,
let me fully share his passion,
precious death on Calvary.

* Alternative to verse 1, line 8: through the passion price he paid

In the fourth verse, 'surging' (line 1), 'to cling' (line 3) and 'fully' (line 7) should be omitted from the descant.

DINIWEIDRWYDD

Welsh tune

3 Pilgrim, fainting in the tempest

Translated from 'Bererin llesg gan rym y stormydd' 8.7.8.7.D. Trochaic

Pilgrim, fainting in the tempest,
lift your gaze where he is found,
see the Lamb, our Mediator,
where his vestments sweep the ground;
faithfulness, his golden girdle;
bells around his hem proclaim
endless mercy for the sinner,
full atonement in his name.

In your feeble state remember:
ankle deep, the stream will rise
like a great unfathomed river,
measured for you in the skies;
only resurrection's children
swim in floods so deep and wide;
fathomless and shoreless waters,
form Bethesda's mighty tide.

O, the depths of our salvation!
Mystery of godliness,
that the God of gods, appearing,
wore our nature and our flesh;
here, in his own person, suffered,
all the anger in our stead,
until justice cried, 'release him!
right is done, atonement made!'

O, eternal rest and rapture,
when I labour here no more,
found within that sea of wonders,
where one never sees a shore;
coming in to life abundant,
where the Three in One is mine;
boundless sea to swim for ever;
One the human and divine!

FALCON WAY

Christopher Maxim (1971-)

4 Though it crosses human nature

Translated from 'Er mai cwbwl groes i natur' 8.7.8.7.D. Trochaic

Though it crosses human nature,
this perplexing path I trace,
I will travel on it calmly,
while I see your precious face;
take the cross as crown and gladly,
through oppression and dismay,
seek the city of fulfilment,
by the straight though tortuous way.

Way, so ancient, never ageing,
Way whose name is Wonderful;
ever new, without beginning,
Way which saves the dying soul;
Way my Spouse and Way my sovereign,
winsome Way, as travellers tell;
consecrated Way, I travel
to my rest beyond the veil.

Way the kite, so keen-eyed, misses,
though it shines with midday light,
Way invisible, untrodden,
only faith perceives the sight;
Way that justifies the godless,
where the dead have life restored,
Way of righteousness for sinners,
peace and favour with the Lord.

Way set up before creation,
then revealed to meet our need,
by the promise made in Eden
which announced the woman's seed;
here the covenant is founded,
here the Three in One's design,
here eternal wine to cheer us,
cheer us, human and divine.

Verse 4, line 1: the red kite, in Ann Griffiths' day common in the skies of Wales, a keen-eyed bird of prey and scavenger, is now beginning to be seen there again.

ARFON *Welsh tune*

5 Comes the day the royal offspring

Translated from 'Mae'r dydd yn dod i'r had brenhinol' 8.7.8.7.D. Trochaic

Comes the day the royal offspring
gain their land across the sea;
after slaving in the brickyards,
share their Father's sovereignty;
faith is there transformed to vision,
hope becomes beatitude,
where they sing faith's endless anthem,
magnify the precious blood.

My heart wants to leave behind it
all the idols of the earth;
I'm inscribed with his own image,
object of far greater worth;
worth unending adoration,
love and praise with every breath:
from death's jaws he has delivered
life for myriads by his death.

Now my precious nard is fragrant,
since I feast on love's free grace,
blaze with zeal against transgression,
love perfection's holy face;
tearing eye and right hand from me,
all my lofty looks cast down:
none else fit to be exalted,
none but Jesus wears the crown.

O, to live now, sanctifying
God's most pure and holy name,
humbled to his will, and making
his command my life's sole aim;
live, to pay my vows completely,
live, to share Christ's treasure store,
where, by his free mercy strengthened,
I am more than conqueror.

Deck me out in your own image,
held, as terror, at your side;
seeing me, let hell, corruption,
godlessness, be terrified;
join me to your name completely,
precious ointment, freely poured,
salt of earth, refreshing fragrance,
gifts to bless the church of God.

MEIRIONYDD *William Lloyd (1786 -1852)*

6 O for the faith, with angels

Translated from 'O am gael ffydd i edrych' 7.6.7.6.D. Iambic

O for the faith, with angels,
to penetrate and see
the plan of our salvation,
its hidden mystery:
two natures in one Person,
conjoined inseparably,
distinct and not confounded,
in perfect unity.

My soul, see this divine one,
how right he is for you;
here venture your whole being,
give him your burdens too.
As human, he feels with you,
your weakness as his own;
as God: the world, flesh, Satan,
are conquered at his throne.

Each day I have a yearning
to leave this field of blood;
not quit the ark, nor Israel,
but self's high surging flood;
to gain my great king's table,
called higher by my host;
though, mean and weak, I only
dared love him from the dust.*

Although the winds blow strongly,
and surging waves come on,
yet Wisdom is the pilot,
his name the Mighty One;
at last, though sin still rises,
corruption still abroad,
we will be safe from danger,
because our ark is God!

* literally 'in the dust'

7 Though the soul in greatest fervour

Translated from 'Pan fo'r enaid mwya gwresog' 8.7.8.7.D. Trochaic

MEREDYDD *Alan Luff (1928-)*

Though the soul in greatest fervour
blazes up with love's own fire,
it can never scale the glory,
God's pure law still reaches higher.
O that I might do it honour:
take Salvation's offered good;
enter into sweet communion,
through immersion in his blood.

Wonder, breeding greater wonder
when that hour completes my joys;
when my mind, that here still wanders
after this world's ailing toys,
through eternal dedication
to this object it adores,
is secure with his great Person,
shaped to heaven's holy laws.

8 What a wonder! to be living

Translated from 'Mae bod yn fyw o fawr ryfeddod' 8.7.8.7.D. Trochaic

BODAWEN *Welsh tune*

What a wonder! to be living,
once to furnace flames consigned;
greater wonder, after testing,
centred here, like gold refined;
time of bleaching, day of sifting,
yet so calm, without distress,
for the one who sifts the harvest,
is himself my hiding place.

Life is weary, I am stricken,
pressed by foes persistently,
coming round like bees and swarming,
day and night, continually;
even some from my own household
lead the hellish war on good,
yet, by grace, I go on fighting,
even though I shed my blood.

TANYCASTELL *The melody by John Jones (Talysarn) (1796-1857)*

9 O, my head should be all waters

Translated from 'O na bai fy mhen yn ddyfroedd' 8.7.8.7.D. Trochaic

O, my head should be all waters,
weeping day and night away:
Zion's army, with its banners,
melts before the heat of day;
O, reveal again the pillars,
mainstay through her night of loss,
God's own promises, unchanging,
sealed supremely on the cross.

Lord, remember your beloved,
leap towards her like a deer;
when Amalakites attack her,
never let them triumph here;
there are foxes prowling round her,
which devour the growing corn;
more and more as daylight passes,
God's Shekinah is withdrawn.

Lord, awake, put on your power,
keep the covenant you gave;
see, your mighty name is hidden,
witnesses are in the grave;
say the Word, great Resurrection,
bring them, living, out of night,
your new name inscribed upon them,
shining like the morning light.

This new name is precious perfume;
by its fragrancy alone,
foes are made love's worthy objects,
cherished by the Three in One;
here repentance has been hidden,
no one can turn back the grace,
till the corn is safely gathered,
evermore in his embrace.

10 Since I still remain corrupted

Translated from 'Am fy mod i mor llygredig' 8.7.8.7.D. Trochaic

MORIAH *Welsh tune*

Since I still remain corrupted,
leaving you repeatedly,
right to scale your sacred mountain
is high privilege to me;
there the veils are torn that hide you
every cover swept aside,
transient things of earth made nothing,
your great glory magnified.

O, to drink on high for ever,
where salvation's waters rise,
drink, till I no longer thirst for
transient things the earth supplies;
live to watch for my Lord's coming,
wide awake and in my place,
there to open quickly to him
and, in joy, reflect his face.

11 I will walk the vale of weeping

Translated from 'Yng nglyn wylofain bydd fy ymdaith' 8.7.8.7.6 7.

PRISCILLA *D. J. James (1743-1831)*

I will walk the vale of weeping,
till I see the blood divine,
streaming from the rock, a river
making many thousands clean;
shining stone, Christ alone
makes his righteousness my own.

I am yearning for that moment
when my privilege, revealed,
in the tree of life Christ Jesus,
by his righteousness is sealed:
steadfast grace makes my case,
in the futile fig-leaf's place!

EDERN *Ian Sharp (1943-)*

12 See him stand among the myrtles

Translated from 'Wele'n sefyll rhwng y myrtwydd' 8.7.8.7.4.7.

See him stand among the myrtles,
object worthy of my mind,
though I only partly know him,
over all things, unconfined;
hail that morning,
when I see him as he is.

He is called the Rose of Sharon,
handsome, radiant, fair of face,
he excels by far ten thousand
splendid sights in time and space;
friend of sinners,
here's their pilot on the sea.

What concern to me in future,
ailing idols of the earth?
I proclaim that none among them
rivals Jesus' matchless worth;
O to stay here,
in his love through all my days.

Verse 1: Zechariah *1:8–11. A mysterious figure whom Ann Griffiths takes to be Christ. See R. S. Thomas, 'Fugue for Ann Griffiths', for his use of these lines.*

Verse 2: Song of Solomon *2:1*.

This hymn may also be sung to LLWYNBEDW *(No. 13).*

13 Do not stare with hesitation

Translated from 'Nac edrychod neb i gloffi' 8.7.8.7.4.7.

LLWYNBEDW *J. T. Rees (1857-1949)*

Reprinted by permission of Morfudd Rhys Clark

Do not stare with hesitation:
I am black, but though the sun
pours its scorching heat upon me
fiery splendour blazing down,
I am sheltered
by the veils of Solomon.

Song of Solomon *1:5–7.*

14 In endless wonder, bride, declare

Translated from 'Rhyfedda fyth, briodas-ferch' LM

LLEDROD (LLANGOLLEN) *Welsh tune*

In endless wonder, bride, declare
yourself the object of his care;
and he whose ransomed seed you are
excels ten thousand souls by far.

15 Earth, with all its trinkets, forfeits

Translated from 'Ni ddichon byd a'i holl deganau' 8.7.8.7.D. Trochaic

Y PREN GWYRDDLAS *Welsh ballad tune arranged Alan Luff (1928-)*

Earth, with all its trinkets, forfeits
my affections from this hour,
which were captivated, broadened,
when my Jesus dawned in power;
he, and nothing less, fulfils me,
he whom mind can not define;
O, to gaze upon his person,
who is human and divine.

O, that I might live to honour
his shed blood, and take my seat,
calmly sheltered in his shadow;
live and die there at his feet;
love the cross, it is my husband's,
lift the cross, endure the load,
and delighting in his Person,
ever worship him as God.

16 The justice table of our God

Translated from 'Ni ddaeth i fwrdd cyfiawnder Duw' CMD

BANGOR

W. Tans'ur
from Harmony of Zion, *1735*

The justice table of our God,
recalling sin, could share
mere shadows of the life and good
that would at last appear;

but on the day of Jubilee
the veil was torn aside;
the law, in Jesus on the tree,
is fully satisfied.

LLANGAN *Welsh tune*

17 When sin's power the first two captured

Translated from 'Pan gymerodd pechod aflan' 8.7.8.7.D. Trochaic

When sin's power the first two captured,
took them from their spotless state,
then the God of Love, by nature,
was himself constrained to hate;
yet these objects of his anger:
still he loved them, set them free;
in a just way, never changing
his complete integrity.

18 Underneath my head, his left hand

Translated from 'Ei law aswy sy'n fy nghynnal' 8.7.8.7.D. Trochaic

Underneath my head, his left hand
bears me through the heat of noon;
while the blessings of his right hand
clasp me, make my soul his own.
I adjure you, nature's posies
beautifying earthly lands,
do not stir unless my Loved One,
my great Glory, so demands.

Song of Solomon 2:6–7

19 O to penetrate the knowledge

Translated from 'O am dreiddio i'r adnabyddiaeth' — 8.7.8.7.D. Trochaic

CWYNFAN PRYDAIN — *Welsh tune arranged David Evans (1874-1948)*

Reprinted by permission of David M. Evans

O to penetrate the knowledge
of the one true living God,
far enough to slay the notions
human fancy has explored;
trust the word which tells his nature:
guilty ones would be destroyed,
if his own atoning mercy,
did not bring us home to God.

In the presence of this knowledge
lofty looks are all cast down;
we, so small and sick and loathsome,
God, the great and holy one;
Christ, in mediating for us,
precious and essential Word,
makes the guilty soul that sees him
glorify his name as God.

20 I'll walk unhurried all my days

Translated from 'Mi gerdda'n ara ddyddiau f'oes' 8.8.8.D.

PEN UCHA *Morfydd Llwyn Owen (1892-1918)*

I'll walk unhurried all my days,
the cross and blood to guard my ways;
I'll run life's course while I have breath
and, running, I will stand to see
where full salvation comes to me,
as I arrive to rest in death.

EIFIONYDD

J. Ambrose Lloyd (1815-74)

21 God is infinite in mercy

Translated from 'Mae'r Duw anfeidrol mewn trugaredd' 8.7.8.7.D. Trochaic

God is infinite in mercy,
God is love, and Love his name,
yet I think of him with terror,
full of grief, distraught with shame;
but within the tent of meeting
he is full of peace and grace:
God enthroned and reconciling,
peace alone found in his face.*

There my food and drink are ready,
my retreat and resting place,
there my healing and my treasure,
mighty tower, essential grace;
there my all-protecting armour
when my hateful foes draw near;
there my life is safely sheltered,
while I fight my battles here.

God as Father; Father, Refuge;
Refuge, Rock and Rock my Tower:
more than this I cannot wish for,
with me through the flood and fire;
now in him I have sufficient,
in this faith I join the fray;
lacking him, weak, feeble, helpless,
I would surely lose the day.

* Alternative to verse 1, line 8: only peace found in his face

CROES ENEURYS *Christopher Maxim (1971-)*

22 Wonder! wonder to the angels

Translated from 'Rhyfedd, rhyfedd gan angylion' 8.7.8.7.D. Trochaic

Wonder! wonder to the angels,
mighty wonder faith perceives:
see life's giver and sustainer,
ruler over all that lives,
lying swaddled in a manger,
with no resting place on earth,
yet the shining host in glory
now adores him at his birth.

When Mount Sinai smokes and trembles,
when the trumpet sounds on high,
I can feast across the limit,
and, in Christ the Word, not die;
all the fulness dwelling in him
fills perdition's emptiness,
here the breach with God is mended,
his self-sacrifice makes peace.

He, the Right, between the robbers,
he endures death's pain and loss;
he who gave the arms that killed him
power to nail him to the cross;
when he pays the debt of firebrands,
fiercely shining Righteousness
honours all his Father's statutes,
freely pardons, pays the price.

Source of peace, and peerless sovereign:
see my soul, where he was laid,
— all creation moving in him —
in the tomb, and with the dead;
life of all the lost, their anthem,
wonder to the seraphim;
seeing God in flesh they worship,
all in chorus, shout 'To Him!'

Verse 2: Exodus *19.10–25*

Part 2

Thanks, ten thousand thanks for ever,
thanks while I have breath to praise;
here's an object for my worship,
theme of song for endless days;
in my nature he was tempted
like the vilest human clod;
human, and a helpless baby,
true, unfathomed, living God.

Shed this body of corruption,
join the fervent choirs on high,
there to penetrate the wonders:
sure Salvation, Calvary;
now I live to see the Unseen,
he who died and lives as Lord,
joined for ever, never parted,
in communion with my God.

There made perfect, in his image
by whom God's atonement came,
far beyond imagination,
I will glorify his name;
I will come into the mystery
opened by his wounds, and then
I will kiss the Son for ever,
never turn from him again!

Alternative tunes: Part 1 HYFRYDOL (Nos. 25–27)
Part 2 MEREDYDD (No. 7) or ARFON (No. 5)

HOPE PARK *Ian Sharp (1943-)*

23 Though I face the surging river

Translated from 'Os rhaid wynebu'r afon donnog' 8.7.8.7.D. Trochiac

Though I face the surging river,*
there is one to break its power:
Jesus, my high priest, is faithful,
in his grasp I am secure;
in his bosom, I cry conquest
over death, world, grave and hell,
ever glorious in his image,
ever sinless, all is well.

Sweet to call to mind the Covenant,
fashioned by the Three in One,
ever gazing on the Person,
who himself became a man;
grieved to death in soul, he finished
all the covenant requires;
now beyond the veil the thousands
sing their song in joyful choirs.

Live where sun no longer scorches,
live where death can come no more;
where all sorrows have been vanquished,
sing the mortal wound he bore;
swim in life's pure flowing river,
peaceful with the Trinity,
under griefless, cloudless glory,
matchless light of Calvary.

* Alternative to verse 1, line 1: If I have to face the river

CLOD *English tune*

VALERY *Alan Luff (1928-)*

24 Make me, my God, just like a tree that grows

Translated from 'Gwna fi fel pren planedig, O fy Nuw' 10 10.10 10. Iambic

Make me, my God, just like a tree that grows
securely planted where life's river flows;
with wide-spread roots and leaves that never fade,
and fruits, from showers your godly wounds have made.

A good land, free of sorrow, well-secured
where flowing milk and honey are assured,
and grapes in bunches picked for desert ways,
a heavenly land, that far exceeds all praise.

Jehovah here, for ever stays the same,
fulfils his promises, confirms his name;
he lifts his hand, to beckon race on race,
and prove the worth of free and boundless grace.

Missions of peace, by gospel tongues released,
across the Indian ocean take the feast,
and Hottentots, Coranian hordes, set free,
Barbarian hosts, all join God's family.

The fourth stanza reflects the concern for overseas mission that was engendered by the 18th-century revival. A similar listing of races appears in the full version of William Williams' English hymn 'O'er those gloomy hills of darkness'. It is usually found best to omit such verses today, and the first three verses make an entirely satisfactory hymn.

HYFRYDOL

R. H. Pritchard (1811-87)
arranged Ralph Vaughan Williams (1872-1958)

Reprinted by permission of Oxford University Press from the *English Hymnal*

Though the three stanzas on the facing page are among those attributed to Ann Griffiths, the attribution is quite uncertain (E. Wyn James).

Although there is no historical link between the stanzas, there is a sufficient movement of thought through them to justify their being sung as one hymn. The second stanza takes up the image of the ark and moves on to the Lamb of Calvary, on whom the last stanza concentrates in adoration.

25 Here is born for us a brother

Translated from 'Dyma Frawd a anwyd inni' 8.7.8.7.D. Trochaic

Here is born for us a brother,
born to share our testing days,
faithful, brimming with compassion,
worthy of increasing praise;
captives freeing, sickness healing,
Zion's straight and holy road,
fountain sparkling, life through dying,
our salvation, ark of God.

26 All the earth's far-spreading oceans

Translated from 'Nid eill y moroedd mawrion llydain' 8.7.8.7.D. Trochaic

All the earth's far-spreading oceans,
cannot hide away our sin,
no tremendous flood can drown it,
it remains alive within;
but the Lamb's blood there on Calvary,
– his just merit, deadly pain –
is the ocean that will hide it,
never to appear again.

27 There can be no earthly object

Translated from 'Nid oes gwrthrych ar y ddaear' 8.7.8.7.D. Trochaic

There can be no earthly object
really precious now to me;
seeing you, my only comfort;
your face, my tranquility;
with you, earthly ties are broken,
every earthly creature's claim;
love and friendship seem as nothing,
for the sake of your great name.

EBENEZER T. J. Williams (1869-1944)

Reprinted by permission of Mrs Dilys Evans

Although there is no historical link between the verses on the facing page, there is a sufficient movement of thought between the verses to justify singing them as one hymn if it is borne in mind that there is a change of voice in the second stanza. The first stanza voices despair at love growing cold and pleads for a revelation: that comes with encouragement in the second: the response in the third stanza is a prayer to remain faithful.

28 Must my zeal, like glowing embers

Translated from 'A raid i'm sêl, oedd farwor tanllyd' 8.7.8.7.D. Trochaic

Must my zeal, like glowing embers,
burning for your glory, Lord,
kindness felt when I was younger,
now go cold towards my God?
Great inhabitant of heaven,
now reveal your joyful face;
from the breasts of this creation
wean my spirit to your grace.

29 Keep on following the reapers

Translated from 'Cofia ddilyn y medelwyr' 8.7.8.7.D. Trochaic

Keep on following the reapers,
spend your life among the sheaves;
when the mount of Sinai blazes,
dip the morsel faith receives;
at the cross, discern God's mystery,
where you tread an altar raise;
God in human nature suffers;
cry for light to sing his praise.

30 Ever in a sea of wonders

Translated from 'Mewn môr o ryfeddodau' 8.7.8.7.D. Trochaic

Ever in a sea of wonders,
O, to stay there, if I could!
Even in this place of sinners,
living by his cross and blood;
with my mind enthralled completely,
wholly subject to Christ's laws,
fashioned like him through obedience,
faithful witness to his cause.

PRYSGOL

William Owen (1813-93)

ing

8.7.8.7.D. Trochaic

ai blazing,*
claimed his law,
vas forfeit,
ed with awe,
ery thundered,
place,
s made foreshadowed
ifice.

attributed to Ann Griffiths, its attribution is far from
orking by John Hughes, Pontrobert, of Hymn 29.

8.7.8.7.D. Trochaic

vation,
ally;
fts of healing,
s free;
fall of Eden,
waters, take
ng virtues,
sda's lake.

nn Griffiths, E. Wyn James points out that it may be a
mn 3.

ic touch to enthronement

"Under the dark trees, there
e stands.
There he stands; shall he not
raw my eyes?
I thought I knew a little.
How he compels, beyond all
nings, but now.
He stands there in the shadows. It will be.
On such a daybreak, such
right morning.
When I shall wake to see him
s he is."

The hymn finishes: "He is a stranger to them all, great Jesus.
What is there here for me? I know.
What I have longed for. Him to hold.
Me always."

The enthronement is to be attended by the Prince of Wales, representing the Queen, and senior ministers. Leaders of other Christian denominations, including Cardinal Cormac Murphy-O'Connor, the Catholic archbishop of Westminster, Joel Edwards, director of the Evangelical Alliance, and the Rev Anthony Burnham, moderator of the Free Churches, will also take part.

Yesterday the new archbishop was introduced to the Church of England's general synod in London, to warm applause and a standing ovation.

After praying for peace and justice, the archbishop quoted the first of his 103 predecessors, St Augustine, saying: "What I am for you troubles me. What I am with you consoles me."

More at guardian.co.uk/religion

25/07/03

PEN YR YRFA

Welsh tune, completed and arranged William James (1877-1964)

Reprinted by permission of Miss Megan James

33 Around the hem of Jesus

Translated from 'Mae sŵn y clychau'n chwarae' 7.6.7.6.D. Iambic

Around the hem of Jesus
the bells are heard to sound;
the scent of pomegranates
is trailed across the ground;
delight is all-pervading,
the sinner justified,
and through the blameless offering,
the Father satisfied.

Exodus *28:33–34*

34 O Lord and God, Salvation

Translated from 'O Arglwydd Dduw rhagluniaeth' 7.6.7.6.D. Iambic

O Lord and God, Salvation,
great Providence, whose throne
stands over earth and heaven;
you rule, and you alone;
in every tribulation
that I have yet to face,
give your strong hand to help me
and shield me with your grace.

Though included among the stanzas attributed to Ann Griffiths this attribution is almost certainly wrong (E . Wyn James).

The Letters of Ann Griffiths

translated by Alan Luff

Introduction to the Letters

These letters are personal and direct, sometimes tumultuous expressions of the day to day feelings of Ann Griffiths at various, mainly unknown points in her life.[1] Occasionally there is the feeling that the letter has been written over a whole day, between household chores, or perhaps even over a longer period still, with John Hughes being addressed anew as she takes up her pen once more. The longer eighth letter flows rather more smoothly and is slightly different in its tone, being written more to a friend and equal, but is not worlds removed. Above all the first seven express her feeling of need for help and guidance, of a kind that she clearly finds that she receives from John Hughes. Spiritual letters from a counsellor to the counselled abound in various Christian traditions. Here we have only the words of the one seeking counsel, such a one, however, as shows profound spiritual insights even when she herself is deeply aware of her own needs. As the poet R. S. Thomas puts it:

> To the traveller up learning's slope:
> "She is ahead of you on her knees".[2]

The letters show that Ann Griffiths may, like many deeply gifted people, have been the subject of what we would today call 'mood swings'. Instead of giving way to this, however, we find her in the letters struggling to set even her darker experiences in the context of the work of God in saving her soul. R. S. Thomas again:

> She described her turbulence
> to her confessor, who was the more
> astonished at the fathoms
> of anguish over which she had
> attained to the calmness of her harbours.

Those moments of peace, of rest, of exaltation as she gazes upon her Saviour are in the hymns. She never learnt, as did the Psalmists, to sing the song of lament.

She infuses her hymns with scripture: in her letters she quotes scripture. Where she quotes from the classic Bishop Morgan translation, I have borrowed the words of the King James' Bible. Her use of scripture, in the letters as in the hymns, is often unexpected, showing how deeply she had wrestled with the words until she is finding in them far more than the ordinary reader might. Derived from the Bible, there is also in the letters the language of contemporary

1 Apart from Letter 8, which exists in Ann Griffiths' own handwriting, the letters have gone through several copying stages that may well, especially at later stages, have included a tidying up of hastily written notes. This is a specialist study, not for this present publication. The present translations are from the texts given by Megan Siân in *Gwaith Ann Griffiths* (1982).

2 *Fugue for Ann Griffiths*: R. S. Thomas. From *Welsh Airs*, published by Seren (1990). Reprinted by kind permission of the author. This is a much longer poem than most of his works and is enlightening for the way that one poet clearly speaks very directly to another. It is to be read after reading Ann Griffiths herself, not as an introduction to her.

spiritual conversation, presumably the language of the Methodist 'Society'. One wonders, did Ann ever recite her hymns there?[3]

There is one, precious, autobiographical note about her hymns as she draws to a close in Letter 8. 'Byth dan ganu' – 'for ever singing' – she writes, with a possibility that indeed 'byth' is 'for eternity'. It is a throw-away phrase: of course she will sing – what else? But that word 'canu', while it certainly means 'sing', has equally strongly the meaning 'compose (a song or hymn)'. So these songs she can imagine herself singing 'byth', include her own amazing hymns, that she takes for granted as they flow naturally from her.

> Here for a few years
> the spirit sang on a bone bough
> at eternity's window, the flesh trembling
> at the splendour of forgiveness
> too impossible to believe in, yet believing.[4]

Cardiff
February 1999

Alan Luff

3 For more background information see Alan Luff, *Welsh Hymns and their Tunes* (1990).
4 R. S. Thomas, op. cit.

Letter 1

28 November 1800

Dear brother,

I have taken this opportunity to send these few lines to you, to show my readiness to receive and answer your substantial letter, and since I certainly believe that it is in the field of Boaz[5] that you have been gleaning the ears of corn so full of blessing that you sent to me, urging me to rub them and to feed upon them; and I think that they have had so much effect on my thoughts as to make me sigh for the Rock,[6] for you could have sent nothing more relevant to my condition at present; that truly was your aim, since you know more about my story in all kinds of misery than does anyone else. I am very glad to hear that you continue in meditation on your own condition and in the Word, and I wish you success in it all. As far as we go in Pontrobert,[7] as far as our bodily health goes, we are as usual; as far as our souls, the society as a body is much more awake, and the ministry under divine unction generally. I have little to say at present about anyone personally; but I would be glad to report what has been happening to me. I have had certain quite bruising trials, and strong winds, to the point that I was about to lose my breath on the hill path; but I believe that I was brought up to the top by the following two chains: 'And a Man shall be as a hiding place from the wind etc';[8] and, 'Come, my people, enter thou into thy chambers, and shut the doors etc';[9] there was quiet and warmth for a while. I have been under another trial, to do with the way I have passed my time in the church of God, coming to the conclusion that my faith from the beginning has had false aims, and thinking to give up: but I was lifted like this, 'Seeing then that we have a great High Priest etc'.[10] But at present I am clouded over and doubtful concerning my own condition; and it beats on my thought whether there has been begun a true work upon me or not; but in the face of everything, this is what I say, 'Though he slay me, yet will I trust in him.'[11]

We had privileges of great worth in recent days; we had the administration of the Lord's Supper twice, and a comforting fragrance on the breaking of bread.

Dear brother, I was glad to hear the point about the circumstances of the church of God, being open to those who profess the faith, since I think that not to be wholly strange to me in these disturbing days of nesting upon Sion. There is special obligation on every Christian who is awake to the matter to mourn when they see the stones of the sanctuary at the head of every street seeming to be whoring and thieving and such. I desire you especially to take the bride of the lamb to the throne of grace; groan much for her restoration; commend her to her bridegroom; for God does not refuse his people that he knew before, because the convenant is a covenant upon oath, even though she is a whore. Two passages of scripture have been on my mind, the one mentioned above, and the other like this, 'In the hand of the Lord there is a cup, and the wine is red; it is full of mixture; and he poureth out of the same: but all the wicked of the earth shall drink the dregs.'[12] There came as dawn upon my mind. For if it happens that one of

5 *Ruth* 3.
6 *1 Corinthians* 10:4.
7 Pontrobert: a hamlet near Dolwar Fach.
8 *Isaiah* 32:2.
9 *Isaiah* 26:20.
10 *Hebrews* 4:14.
11 *Job* 13:15.
12 Psalm 75:8.

the cups that are spoken of is poured out, the children will be but purged, because it is in the hand of a father. But let us pray much for help to endure the medicine, be it as bitter as it may be to restore us.

For the moment I shall come to an end; and this is from your fellow pilgrim journeying towards eternity.

Ann Thomas
Dolwar

Letter 2

17 February 1801

Dear brother in the Lord,

I have taken the opportunity to send these lines to you to let you know that I have received your letters with affection, hoping that the weighty things that are in them will find place in my thought. I am glad to be able to hear how things are with you with regard to your condition. It is precious to have a friend that cleaves to you, as you have said.

A word has remained on my mind that it might be good for me to mention on this subject, 'Simon, Son of Jonas, lovest thou me more than these?'[13] I have thought that one needs to go beyond brethren and graces, and to love the Giver above the gift. There was another word remained on my mind, 'Buy the truth, and sell it not.'[14] It came to my mind that I am content to give all that I possess, my good and my bad, for the Son in marriage union. My thought is that every idle word and all levity of spirit, and all behaviour that seems to be contrary to holiness, entirely denies that we know Jesus Christ. But in the face of our great wretchedness, how precious it is to think on that word, 'The Lord turned and looked upon Peter.'[15]

I am cheered to think that there is freedom for the sinner to speak so much about Jesus Christ at the throne of grace; the heavens smiling and hell quaking. Let us make much of our privilege that we have known something of the effects of the blessings of the eternal covenant that is ordained above. Oh, to be allowed to remain beneath the drops from the sanctuary until the evening, and to acknowledge that they are the price of blood, which fells sinners to the dust. Oh, to be at the feet of our good God while we live in the world!

Further, I can send you a little of how things are with the Society in Pontrobert. In general it is experiencing the dew of blessing, and is quite awakened. As concerns most of the church at the moment, my thought is that she is no stranger to the wine that is shared among the Disciples here on their journey. If I am to say what is happening to me, I desire to speak well of God, that he remembers me in the face of many doubts. I have never seen so much cause to cry aloud concerning the Rock in all weather, and whether dead or alive, this is my cry, Oh, to be found in him, without any of my own righteousness that comes from the law!

I heard a similitude, about a shopkeeper going to a city to buy two hundred pounds worth of goods; that he had the bill for that parcel hanging in the shop, names and amounts of his property on it; and that a man comes in and asks for a crown's worth of one of them. He answers that he does not own one pennyworth of it. Though many can appear grand in their profession

13 *John* 21:15.
14 *Proverbs* 23:23.
15 *Luke* 22:61.

of faith, yet in the face of hardship, ask where is their faith? Little children cried out, Shout for the cart to come home laden from the market; that is, the ministers of the word.

For the moment I shall come to an end: and this is from one who longs to wish success to those on the way to Zion.

Ann Thomas
Dolwar

Letter 3

Dear brother,

I have taken this opportunity to write to you, hoping that you are well and to let you know that I have received your valuable letter. I beg you not to neglect to send helpful things to me, taking no notice of our neglectfulness, since you know the reason, that I have hardly anything of worth to send.

Beloved brother, I would be glad to see you many times in the midst of my distress of mind, suffering as I do gnawing doubts concerning the truth of the visitations, and the revelation of the Mediator, to a greater or lesser degree despite my damnable and lost state. And though I have tried many paths and failed to attain to my purpose, except for the way of meditation. There is a lesson from that which the father-in-law of Moses advised him: to set sixty elders to judge the people requiring ordinary insight, but to bring the large, obscure matters to him.[16] I thought that my perplexing state should go beyond the watchers of the cities and everyone else, to God alone. I have comfort in this when my condition is dark: for me and for my brethren, there is a clear light in the court of the High Priest. Eternal thanks for this.

I gained much pleasure in meditating on the Shunamite woman setting aside a room on the wall for the man of God to rest in when he came by, placing a bed, a table, a stool and a candlestick.[17] It could be that the woman in her longing for the prophet often paced the room and was cheered while waiting for the man. But however that may be, it is a comfort to the heart of a believer, in the absence of the sight of the face of his Lord, that the furniture is left behind, for a variety of considerations: for one thing, it is a sign that he has not given up; for another it is a lodging too hot for the devil. When the enemy comes in like a strong river, the Spirit of the Lord will chase him away. He cannot so much as lift up his head in the temple of God without quaking, nor look upon anything in it but the marks of his own feet without dismay. For this reason, we cry aloud for the Holy Spirit to make his home in our hearts as we are.

Beloved brother, it is a dark time at present for the church in Pontrobert, beneath the onslaughts of the world and of backsliders. I took great pleasure one night confronting these things as I thought what the Holy Spirit says of the church; two passages of scripture were on my mind, 'Glorious things are spoken of thee, O city of God';[18] 'the Lord thy God is strong in the midst of thee.'[19]

Thus much for the present from your sister.

Ann Thomas
Dolwar

16 *Exodus* 18:17–26.
17 *2 Kings* 10.
18 Psalm 87:3.
19 Psalm 46:5.

Letter 4

Dear brother,

I have been glad many times to write to you about how things are with me. I have had much pleasure and blessing from reading your letters; that is what causes me earnestly to desire that you should not withhold your hand. Dear brother, the warfare is as hot now as ever, enemies within and enemies without; but of them all, the sin of the mind is what crushes me most heavily. I am especially glad to think today on that word, 'And to Jesus, the Mediator of the New Covenant, and to the blood of the sprinkling':[20] it is something new to love the teaching of the cleansing. That word is on my mind, 'the blood of Jesus Christ, his son, cleanseth us from all sin'.[21] I had never a greater longing to be pure. That word is on my mind, ' The house, when it was in building, was built of stone made ready before it was brought thither.'[22] Sometimes I think that I do not want ever to change my raiment, but I crave to be clean in my raiment. It would be right for me to be able to stay more in the sanctuary in the way you have spoken of, in a manner more abundant and precious. I am expecting some hard weather to meet me, though I do not know what. That word is tonight on my mind, 'by this therefore shall all the iniquity of Jacob be purged.'[23] Oh for help to stay with God whatever shall confront me, and thanks for ever that the furnace and the fountain are so close to one another!

There is nothing more that is especially on my mind at the moment, but remember me often and hurry to send to me. I will add no more at the moment. I am your unworthy sister who loves your success in body and soul.

Ann Thomas
Dolwar

Letter 5

Beloved brother in the Lord,

I am writing to you at this present moment because the inclination of my mind, in the face of hard weather of every kind, is to give an account of myself to you, dear brother.

Dear brother, the most special thing that is on my mind is that I feel greatly bound to be thankful to the Lord for holding me safe in face of the winds and floods. I can say that my thoughts have never been gripped by such a measure of fears as in these days. But in the face of it all I think to hang quietly upon that precious promise, 'when thou passest through the waters, I will be with thee.'[24] I think that he is sufficient to support me between the meeting of two seas.[25] Thanks be for ever to God who is so full of promises.

Dear brother, the thing that is most pressing upon my mind at the present is the sin that any thing in this world of sight should take first place in my mind. I am reverently ashamed, and rejoice in astonishment, at the thought that the one for whom it is a condescension to behold the things that are in heaven,[26] has given himself to be an object of love to a creature as base as I.

20 *Hebrews* 12:24.
21 *1 John* 1:7.
22 *1 Kings* 6:7.
23 *Isaiah* 27:9.
24 *Isaiah* 43:2.
25 Acts 27:41.
26 Psalm 113:6.

In the face of it being such a dishonour to God to give the foremost place to things of second rank, this simply is my thought: if it is necessary for nature to be crushed into the grasp of death because of its being too weak to bear the bright beams of the sun of afflictions, I think sometimes that I can look gladly to being despoiled of my natural life (if necessary) rather than that glory should go behind a cloud while nature and its idols parade its pomp.

That word is on my mind tonight, 'Go forth, O ye daughters of Zion, and behold King Solomon with the crown wherewith his mother crowned him in the day of his espousals, and in the day of the gladness of his heart.'[27] I think it to be a high and especial call to the whole family of the covenant to go forth from their own boarded houses to see their King 'wearing the crown of thorns, and the purple robe.'[28] It is no wonder that the sun hid its rays when its Creator was pierced by nails. It is a wonder to me to think who it was upon the cross: the one whose eyes are as a flame of fire,[29] piercing through the heavens and the earth, and at the same moment unable to see his creatures, the work of his two hands. My mind is drowning in too great an excess of wonder to say anything more on this. But looking at the greatness of the Person, it is no wonder that that word is set down: 'The Lord is well pleased for his righteousness' sake; he will magnify the law, and make it honourable.'[30]

Dear brother, it is no wonder that that word is set down. 'Kiss the Son lest he be angry.'[31]

Dear brother, there is nothing special upon my mind to enlarge upon at present. But I will say this in drawing to a close: I desire that the part of life that is left to me should be in communion so close that it will not ever be mine ever to say again, 'I will go and I will return.' For my part I think, that if I but have this, that I am content to meet with providence in his wrath and his crosses.

I ask for a special place in your prayers. Remember to send quickly. I am longing for a letter. I am your loving sister.

Ann Thomas
Dolwar

Letter 6

Dear brother and father in the Lord,

I received your letter yesterday and I was very happy to get it, since I hope that the valuable things in it will be of blessing to me. I was very glad of the Scripture on which you commented in my brother's letter; but I would like to go on to tell a little of how matters are faring with me.

I have had a tempestuous passage for some time, having very many disappointments in myself continually. But I must say this, that every trial, all the storms of every kind work together upon me to this end: that is, to draw me to see more of the Lord in his goodness and unchangeableness towards me. I have recently been far gone in spiritual whoring away from the Lord; and yet holding up my head before the ministrations of the church as one who is keeping house well and remaining in the fellowship. But in spite of all my devices, the Lord broke upon me with these words, 'If I am a Father, where is my honour? If I am a Master, where is my fear?' Eternal thanks for the pills of heaven to send the sickness on its way. My stomach was so weak

27 *Song of Solomon* 3:11.
28 *John* 19:5.
29 *Revelation* 2:18.
30 *Isaiah* 42:21.
31 Psalm 2:12.

that I could not feed upon the free mercy. With my path before me, and having departed from God the fountain of all real comforts, and having dug for myself broken wells, that word raised me a little onto my feet once more, 'The Lord is my shepherd; I shall not want'.[32] It is I who am going astray; he the shepherd, and I unable to return; he the Lord Almighty, the rock of our salvation, wholly reliant on himself in the matter of saving the sinner.

Beloved brother, for my part I desire to undergo his treatment, be that as bitter as it may be. Another word has been of special blessing to me recently as I try to voice my complaint to the Lord about the varied things that were tempting me to follow them; here is the word, 'Look unto me and be saved, all the ends of the earth; for I am God and there is none other,'[33] as if God is saying, 'I know of every call upon you, and that each one is different; but I also am calling. The world is nothing but world, and the flesh but flesh, and the devil but devil: but I am God, and there is none other.' I am greatly bound to be thankful for the word in its unconquerable authority. I desire from my heart to give the whole praise to the God of the word alone, that he has nurtured and sustained me thus far, and that the part of life that remains should be in continual communion with God in his son, since I cannot ever glorify him more than by believing and accepting his son. May heaven help me to do this, not for the sake of my own pleasure alone, but out of reverence to him.

Beloved brother, there is hardly anything more on my mind to enlarge upon. But remember greatly in your prayers Zion throughout the world, but especially your mother church in Pontrobert. The shades of evening are almost enveloping her, and grey hair is spreading over her and in small measure she knows it. That word is much on my mind and others too as I look upon her feeble, slovenly and disheartened appearance, 'Is this Naomi?'[34] Labour greatly with the Lord in prayer on our behalf as a body of witnesses for God in the world, because his great name is being besmirched by our backsliding.

Beloved brother, I am glad to hear what is going on in your new work. Two passages of scripture have been on my mind in this connection; one, 'Thus shall it be done to the man whom the king delighteth to honour.'[35] And the other, 'Surely the Lord's anointed is before me; but the Lord seeth not as man seeth.'[36] For this reason it was necessary to fetch David.

For the moment I will draw to a close, desiring you to send to me soon. I am your unworthy sister who is swifly running to the world that endures for ever.

Ann Thomas
Dolwar

Letter 7

Dear brother,

I am sending these lines to you to tell you that I have received your kind letter with affection, and I am glad to have the opportunity to tell you news of my present condition.

Dear brother, I have never conversed with you nor written to you in a more pitiful state than is mine at the moment, and I am ashamed to think that I ever thought differently of myself. This

32 Psalm 23:1.
33 *Isaiah* 45:22.
34 *Ruth* 1:19.
35 *Esther* 6:9.
36 *1 Samuel* 16:6–7.

word came into my mind, 'I have set before you an open door that none can close; for you have a little strength.'[37] Thanks be for ever to the God of all grace for taking his precious word in his hand in his dealings with me: I reverently believe that so it is, and that his axes and their blows are continually upon the root of self-conceit that is so strong in my corrupt nature. There was made plain to me more of my doomed condition some days ago than in the whole period of my profession of faith, and more of the glory of the wise rule of God in justifying the godless, and that he is in Christ reconciling the world to himself, not accounting their sins to them.[38] I am often at the throne of grace, in wonder, thanks and prayer: in wonder that the word and the Holy Spirit have found a way to treat the condition of such an unclean wretch, full of every deceit, without slaying me. Thanks be for the lawfulness of the way of salvation; and that it glorifies its Author, more than that it rewards its travellers. I am praying to be able to spend the rest that remains of my days in a life of communion with God in his son Jesus Christ, the great Mediator between God and men. It would be very precious to me to be delivered from venturing to offer more to the holy law of God than that which has satisfied it; not because it will not accept anything else, but out of respect for it. I have not before known so much respect for the law, and love towards it; not *although* it curses, but *because* it curses in every place except with the Saviour; for so it shows its beauty and perfection.

Beloved brother, I was glad to read the letter you sent to my brother, and also your letter to SG,[39] and your exhortations to read and search the scriptures. I think, in regard to whatever we might have besides the word, and that which might be in accord with it, that we are 'spending money on that which is not bread, and our toil on that which does not satisfy':[40] for the stomach of the new nature does not put up with anything else; and every wind brings sickness, save for the wind of the sanctuary.

The following words have been of worth and great comfort to my soul recently, that is, 'Thy neck is like the tower of David, builded to be an armoury; whereon there hang a thousand bucklers, all shields of mighty men.'[41] I am not, in myself, anything but impotent and defenceless to face enemies; but if I may have the privilege of turning to the tower, I shall have there armour and strength to run through the army. These words too have been of great comfort to me, 'For it pleased the Father that in him should all fullness dwell';[42] and also these words, 'A garden inclosed is my sister and my spouse.'[43] There are heavy obligations upon me to speak well of God, and to be grateful to him for a degree of the fellowship of the mystery. But this is my grief – being unable to stay – continually departing. I see my loss to be great because of this; but the dishonour and disrespect toward God is more than that. Help to stay! This word is often on my mind, 'Meditate on these things; give thyself wholly to them.'[44] I beg you to send me your view on that word, 'In all points tempted like as we ourselves, yet without sin.'[45]

The poor state of the cause of God in a number of places these days presses grievously on my mind. There are heavy obligations on every wakeful soul to struggle greatly with God in fervent prayer, that he should send the winds to blow upon his withered garden, that its perfumes

37 *Revelation* 3:8.
38 *2 Corinthians* 5:19.
39 Miss Sarah Griffiths. She was from Pontrobert.
40 *Isaiah* 55:2.
41 *Song of Songs* 4:4.
42 *Colossians* 1:19.
43 *Song of Songs* 4:12.
44 *1 Timothy* 4:12.
45 *Hebrews* 4:15.

should be diffused; so that Satan and all the subjects of his kingdom should lose their breath by the force of those perfumes.

Now, to draw to a close, I desire you to remember me at the throne of grace. I desire you to send to me at the first opportunity.

This is from one who journeys speedily through the world of time to the world that endures for ever.

Ann Thomas
Dolwar

Letter 8

Dearest sister in the Lord,

At your request I have written these few lines to you and I am glad to have the opportunity to make known to you how things are with me.

Beloved sister, the subject most special on my mind at the present concerns grieving the Holy Spirit. That word came to my mind, 'Know ye not that your body is the temple of the Holy Ghost, which is in you.'[46] As I penetrate a little into the wonders of the Person and that he lives or dwells in the believer, I think simply that I have never been seized to the same degree by reverent fears lest I should grieve him; and with that I was able to see that one cause, and the chief cause, why this great sin has so little pressing influence on my thought is because of my low and blasphemous thoughts about so great a person. This is the way my thoughts ran on the persons of the Trinity. I feel my mind caught in shame, yet bound to speak because of the injury of it, in thinking of the person of the Father and the Son as co-equal, but of the person of the Holy Spirit as if he were a functionary subordinate to them. Oh, what a fanciful and heretical thought concerning a divine person, all-present, all-knowing and almighty to be able to bring forward the good work he began, in the dispensation of free grace and the counsel of the three in one for the objects of the primeval love! Oh to have the privilege of being of their number!

Dear sister, I am feeling a kind of thirst to ascend yet more in belief in the personal presence of the Holy Spirit in my situation; and that, through revelation, not by imagination, thinking to comprehend the manner and means that it comes to be, which would be true idolatry.

Dear sister, looking a little at the sinfulness in itself of grieving the Holy Spirit, and from the other side, looking at the depths of the great fall, and that I am dispossessed of all ability to do anything but grieve him, it is a great weight upon me. But this word is on my mind, 'Watch and pray,'[47] as if the Lord were saying, ' Though the commandment is so severe, and you unable to accomplish one part in a thousand on that ground as far as your mind is concerned, come into the field, make proof of the throne of grace, for "the effectual fervent prayer of a righteous man availeth much,"[48] – "my grace is sufficient for thee; for my strength is made perfect in weakness."'[49] Thanks be to God who is full of promises.

Dear sister, I would wish to say much about the efficacy of private prayer, but you know more than I can say about it; but I am wholly of the opinion that it greatly surpasses a host of armed men in facing enemies. I know from experience what it is to be so surrounded by enemies

46 *1 Corinthians* 6:19.
47 *Mark* 13:33.
48 *James* 5:16.
49 *2 Corinthians* 12:9.

that I can do nothing but that – 'I give myself unto prayer,'[50] and that anwers the purpose so that they fall flat on their backs. Oh to have the privilege of being under the strict oversight of the Holy Spirit! I simply think that no oversight less strict than that word will fit my condition, 'I will water it at every moment.'[51] Eternal thanks for a Bible that fits a condition that has sunk so low. Dear sister, it is a kind of great privilege that such a condition can be held up to the presence of the word of God. Oh to be able to hold it in the holy mirror so as to make use of a Mediator!

One special thing was on my mind last night to do with finding my condition in the word. R.J. speaks in a very valuable way about matters,[52] while I am so dry, so far as my experience goes, that neither law nor gospel was having any effect on me and this brought a measure of fear upon my thought, that I should fail to think to find my condition in the word because the law and the gospel are as without profit to me. That word came to me, 'Go thy way forth by the footsteps of the flock,'[53] with myself failing to see the footprints of the flock in that circumstance. But that word came to my mind with light and warmth, 'Awake, O north wind; and come, thou south.'[54] Thanks be for ever for the rock of the word on which a foot can be placed upon setting out, and the impossibility of setting out without that.

Dear sister, I see more need than I saw ever before to be able to spend what life is left to me in placing myself daily and continually, body and soul, into the care of him who is able to keep what is given to him until that day.[55] Not giving myself once; but living in giving myself, until the time and at the time that I lay this tabernacle aside. Dear sister, the thought of putting it aside is sometimes especially sweet. I can say that it is this that cheers my mind more than anything these days; not dying itself, but the great gain that is to be gained through death; to be able to lay aside every inclination to dishonour the law of God, every weakness being swallowed up by strength, to obtain complete conformity with the law, which is already the desire of my heart, and to enjoy the likeness of God for ever. Dear sister, I am so swallowed up sometimes in these things, that I cannot properly stand on the path of my duty in temporal affairs; but I wait for the time to be freed, and be with Christ, for that is far better,[56] even though I am very happy here sometimes through the lattice, and the Lord reveals as much of his glory, through a mirror in parable, as my weak faculties can bear.

Dear sister, I am glad to say in drawing to a close – I wish to say it with thanksgiving – that despite my whole depravity, and the device of hell, the world and things within it, by the goodness of God alone, I have not changed the object of my love up till this night. But rather I intend from my heart to rest in his love, and to delight in it, always singing, though I shall not attain to it this side of death even to the least degree to encourage me, except through strife.

Dear, beloved sister, I desire you especially to send to me soon; do not disappoint me; I cannot but take it unkindly of you if you do. Ruth wishes me to remember her lovingly to you. I have nothing especially to send to you as news but this; there is a spirit clutching at every hope to see signs of the recovery of Rachel Pugh. This from your beloved sister who is swiftly travelling through the world of time to the world that lasts for ever.

50 Psalm 109:4.
51 *Isaiah* 27:3.
52 Thought to be Richard Jones of the Wern, or Robert Jones, Rhos-lan.
53 *Song of Solomon* 1:8.
54 *Song of Solomon* 4:16.
55 *2 Timothy* 1:12.
56 *Philippians* 1:23.

Index of English First Lines

Index of Welsh First Lines

Index of Tunes

Index of Composers, Arrangers and Sources